Chaim Gross

Sixty Years of Sculpture

A MEMORIAL EXHIBITION

CURATED BY BARBARA S. KRULIK

IN COLLABORATION WITH

THE CHAIM GROSS STUDIO MUSEUM

526 LA GUARDIA PLACE, NEW YORK, NY

October 27 — November 26, 1994

Forum Gallery

745 Fifth Avenue at 57th Street, New York 10151

212/355-4545   FAX 212/355-4547

Chaim Gross

Sixty Years of Sculpture

By Roberta K. Tarbell

CHAIM GROSS (1904–91) will always be remembered for his wood carvings. He was especially sensitive to the unique qualities of various woods because his earliest memories centered on the shapes, colors, and smells of freshly cut wood.[1] His father and other family members, lumbermen by day, passed leisure hours together whittling functional and fanciful wood objects by the light of log fires. Gross' childhood in the idyllic beauty of the mountains and forests of Austria was abruptly curtailed when in 1914 he watched invading Russian Cossacks draw their sabers and assault his parents, an attack which effectively destroyed the integrity of their family. Long after he had emigrated to New York in 1921, Gross associated wood carvings with the peace and self-confidence of his cohesive, extended family in Austria which had enjoyed the stability of centuries of shared Chasidic Judaism, intellectual pursuits, and life-sustaining, satisfying occupations.

From 1921 to 1926, years Gross studied art in New York at the Educational Alliance, the Beaux-Arts Institute of Design, and the Art Students League, he learned about formal abstraction of the human figure and the importance of folk and tribal arts and of wood sculpture from two of the leading modern sculptors in America — Elie Nadelman and Robert Laurent, who, like Chaim Gross, had spent their youthful years in Europe before emigrating to New York. These sculptors, and other European-born modernists, were especially receptive to a wide range of international arts and reflect the coexistence of nativist and foreign influences in their own art in part because they themselves were the products of the traditions of two continents.

The sculptures on view at the two sites of the Chaim Gross Memorial Exhibition include the abstracted wood and stone direct carvings that define his early mature style. He responded strongly to sculptures created by African tribesmen which like his are predominantly totemic, reductive, and axial.[2] His earliest carvings of the late 1920s embrace the solid, compact, roughly hewn log-like qualities of tribal sculptures and herald his lifelong commitment to the technique and aesthetic philosophies of direct carving. He was inspired by the grain, the color, and the texture of the hardest and densest woods — ebony, lignum vitae, mahogany, cocobolo, ipilwood, palo blanco, and walnut.

Allegiance to direct carving determines the peculiar, elongated cylindrical compositions of so many of Chaim Gross' sculptures on view — oriented either horizontally like *Lesbians* (1938), *Swimmer* (1944), and *Mother and Daughter Floating* (1949) or vertically like *I Found my Love* (1948) or his many multifigured stacks of acrobats. Gross must have liked such inhuman tall and narrow dimensions, because he chose wood blocks that exaggerate the normal proportions of the human figure more often than other direct carvers did. In like manner, Gross also selected large boards relatively narrow in depth for many flat, relief-like designs, exemplified by *Offspring* (1930), *Happy Mother* (1931), *Acrobatic Performers* (1932), and *Hoover and Roosevelt in a Fistfight* (1932). The last-mentioned sculpture, of all those in the current exhibition, is the one that most overtly works with the Cubist forms of Picasso and Lipchitz. Gross was aware of the enormous formal vocabulary of modern sculpture, but rarely demonstrated it so self-consciously in his own works.

His choice of the subjects of circus performers and dancers for about one quarter of his wood carvings and of a primitivist, anti-classicizing style place him in the mainstream of modern art. His itinerant entertainers in sculpture, like Picasso's painted harlequins and saltimbanques, although alienated from the middle class socially, control audiences by evoking admiration or laughter from them at will. For Gross, this shared enjoyment, like the sensual qualities of wood, recalled the family camaraderie of his childhood. Both Picasso and Gross, as poor, often misunderstood immigrants, identified with peripatetic performers. Gross emphasized the athletic skills of the acrobats and the ritualistic nature of performance which he arrested in the stopped-action, happy-faced masks of his wooden circus artists. Gross knew that totem poles represent spiritual bonds of tribal or family unity and unintentionally suggested this iconography in stacking acrobats three and four high [totem-like]. He even named one six-foot lignum vitae carving *Circus Totem* (1946).

Another signature genre by Chaim Gross is his series of remarkable wood carvings of statuesque and stately female figures sensuous in the sexuality of their subjects and in the beauty of their materials. Gross caressed and polished these woods, enhancing the richness of the variegated grain of the lignum vitae of *Tightrope Dancer* (1933), the gleaming surfaces of the earthy-toned ebony of *Black Figure* (1935), *Girl Praying* (1944), and *Lot's Wife* (1951), and the rich burnt sienna of the Honduras mahogany he chose for such monumental sculptures as *Bride* (1949) and *Victoria* (1951). The male nude figure is absent in his oeuvre. His celebration of women as the central icon of art is as old as sculpture itself.

Jewish subject matter did not appear in Chaim Gross' art until after World War II when the atrocities of the Holocaust in general and the awareness that the Nazis had exterminated two siblings and a niece caused him to embrace his theological heritage directly in his art. *Sarah* (1956) has a dual reference to the loyal wife of Abraham, sometimes referred to as "the mother of nations," and to his sister, Sarah, who had been victim to the Germans and whose memorial he had first carved in 1947. *Lot's Wife* (1951), who is otherwise unnamed in Genesis, is one of seven variations of this subject Gross carved between 1950 and 1957. In contrast to the faith and humility of the Biblical Sarah, Lot's wife traditionally has been interpreted as a symbol of hedonism and lack of Godliness. *Naomi and Ruth* (1956), like *Sarah*, has both Judaic and familial importance to the sculptor. Ruth, great-grandmother of King David, was the heroic subject of a scriptural book, but she also represents the loyalty and love of family that was so important to Chaim Gross.

The slightly curved and feminine forms of three alabaster sculptures, *Reflection* (1954), *Loving Mother* (1948), and *Adolescents Asleep* (1947), remind me of the carvings of Robert Laurent less because Gross was emulating his teacher's style and more because the nature of the material dictates certain formal properties. Laurent had a special affinity for alabaster and carved fifty sculptures in it. Although Gross carved fewer, the results were similar. The relatively small ovoid blocks of this quarried, soft, gypseous stone lends itself to small, compact sculptures unpierced by voids. Because the chalky crust of unfinished alabaster is opaque, it refracts light; both Gross and Laurent coaxed out the gleaming surfaces and the natural pink translucency of alabaster by rubbing and polishing off the dead outer skin to allow light to penetrate. Like these three alabaster carvings, the subject of many of Gross' carvings in stone were two female figures, usually family members. *Sisters at Play* (1942) in onyx and *Eternal Mother* (1945) of Lithium stone are typical. Although Gross selected the hardest woods to carve, he favored softer stones (alabaster, marble, sandstone, and limestone), which he frequently discovered at demolition sites.

At the age of fifty, after a quarter century of being a prolific carver of sculptures in stone and wood, Chaim Gross began to model full-scale maquettes in plaster for sculptures in bronze. Although he retained his signature subjects of acrobats interacting with each other or mothers playing with their children, his formal approach changed dramatically. When Chaim Gross modeled sculptures in clay or in plaster on an armature, he vigorously exploited the open space and the ability (inherent in the medium) to extend forms in three dimensions at will, as if to counteract the limits in formal options he had encountered for so long in direct carving. Where his carvings were compact, unpierced, softly rounded, closed forms, the plans of the open forms of his bronze sculptures were faceted, angular, and sharp-edged. In their greater angularity and abstraction, they appear more modern than many of his carvings, and in their monumental scale and resistant material, they are more appropriate for the public sites where so many of them have found homes.

Chaim Gross' large retrospective exhibition of 200 works at the Jewish Museum in 1977 catalyzed his renewed interest in carving wood. Many of his carvings of the eighties echo his earliest works but on a larger scale — no minor feat when the material is lignum vitae, the hardest wood known. *Soho Princess with Hat* of 1984 is a hybrid of his female genre and nude figurative carvings fifty years earlier. His unfinished final work (1988–89) appears clothed — reminiscent of his *Madame and Child* of 1939 — but, if Gross had finished *Young Woman*, he might have carved away her mahogany garments to reveal a nude figure underneath as he had with another version of his Soho princess.

For seventy years Chaim Gross contributed as greatly and as dynamically to the city's arts and culture as it had furthered his own development. New Yorkers are familiar with his monumental public sculptures in bronze — *Mother Playing* at Fordham University (Lincoln Center, on Columbus Avenue near 60th Street), *Acrobat in the Ring* and *Heaven and Earth* installed at Pace University (on Gold Street, near City Hall Park, just south of the Brooklyn Bridge), and *The Family* at the Bleeker Street Sitting Area in Greenwich Village. The Jewish Museum, the Metropolitan Museum of Art, and the Museum of Modern Art regularly display his sculptures from their collections. For the past sixty-five years, his work has been frequently exhibited in group and solo exhibitions. From 1927 to 1989 he annually taught hundreds of students in classes at the Educational Alliance, the New School, and various other schools of art in the city. His contributions to the cultural vigor of New York was often private and personal. During Jacques Lipchitz's first week in New York in 1941, for example, Gross offered him the tools and the space to create sculpture. Countless people can testify to this kind of compassion and generosity that were an essential part of Chaim Gross.

Chaim Gross' life and art represent many paradoxes. He was both European and American, and consciously emulated qualities of African art in his own. His sculptures were simultaneously traditional and modern. He embodied in his carvings both the unselfconscious handcraftsmanship of folk and tribal art and the enlightened sophistication of the international avant-garde of the 1920s and 1930s; he mastered the technical complexities of large-scale bronze casts. He was absolutely enmeshed in the dynamic qualities of schools, museums, and organizations of art in New York, the primary urban art center of his time, but also was inspired by the lonely ever-changing nature ambient to his summer home in Cape Cod. He can be categorized with groups of innovative direct carvers, modernist figurative sculptors, and Jewish artists, but he also was fiercely individual and his style is idiosyncratic. He was intellectually open to new ideas and was determined to define in his art the special qualities of human beings in his time and place, yet was aware that art, to be eternal, needed to reflect traditional wisdom. He lived subjectively in his world, but also observed it objectively as an outside observer. His life was finite, but his sculptures will endure forever.

ENDNOTES

1 My in-depth knowledge of the art, life, and aesthetics of Chaim Gross were gained through a series of interviews with him in 1976 and 1977 and reported in part in Tarbell, *Chaim Gross, Retrospective Exhibition: Sculpture, Paintings, Drawings, Prints* (New York: The Jewish Museum, 1977).
Direct carvers like Chaim Gross examined various stone and wood sculptures for technical as well as stylistic insights. Gross was an expert on the properties and characteristics of tropical woods, introduced Alexander Calder and many other sculptors to them, and published a book on the subject [*The Technique of Wood Sculpture* (New York: Vista House, 1957 and Arco Publ. Co., 1966)]

2 Chaim Gross amassed more than 1,000 African objects in wood and metal. See Arnold Rubin, *The Sculptor's Eye: The African Art Collection of Mr. and Mrs. Chaim Gross,* exh. cat. (Washington, D.C.: Museum of African Art, 1976). Gross was a benefactor and founding trustee of the museum for which his friend and protégé, Warren M. Robbins, was founder and first director.

Profile Bird, 1926
MAHOGANY
24½"H X 7"W X 2"D

Jazz, 1929

MAHOGANY

41⅝"H X 17"W X 2¼"D

Private Collection

Two Torsos, 1929
MAHOGANY
27"H X 13"W X 15"D

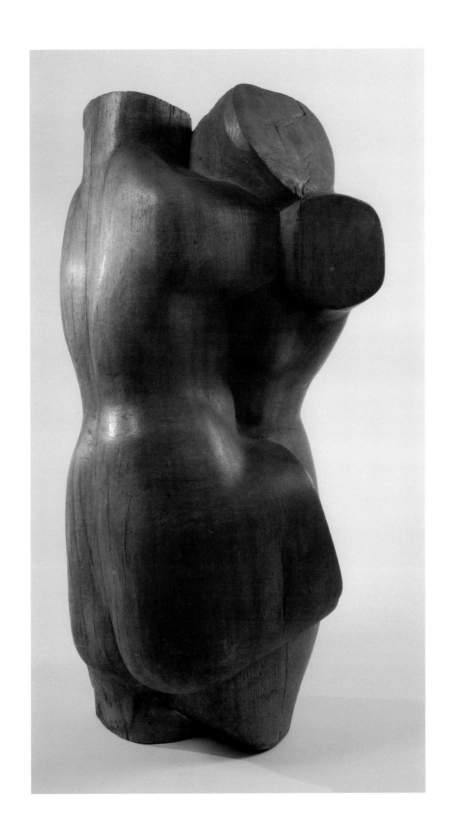

Leap Frog, 1931
LIGNUM VITAE
16"H X 7"W X 6½"D

Rooster, 1931

INDIAN BOXWOOD

21"H X 8"W X 12"D

Acrobatic Performers, 1932
BIRDS-EYE MAPLE
42½"H X 29"W X 1¼"D

Hoover and Roosevelt in a Fistfight, 1932
MAHOGANY
75"H X 21"W X 1½"D

Tightrope Dancer, 1933
LIGNUM VITAE
30"H X 9½"W X 8"D

Pumpkin, 1933

LIGNUM VITAE

7½"H X 12"W X 9"D

Black Figure, 1935
EBONY
40½"H X 12"W X 8"D

Lesbians, 1938
LIGNUM VITAE
7"H X 30"L X 5"D

Acrobats Balancing, 1938
LIGNUM VITAE
34"H X 8½"W X 10½"D

Trapeze Girl, 1938

LIGNUM VITAE

30½"H X 11½"W X 8"D

Madame and Child, 1939
SABICU WOOD
74"H X 20½"W X 18"D

Bird's Nest, 1940

LIGNUM VITAE

49"H X 10"W X 10"D

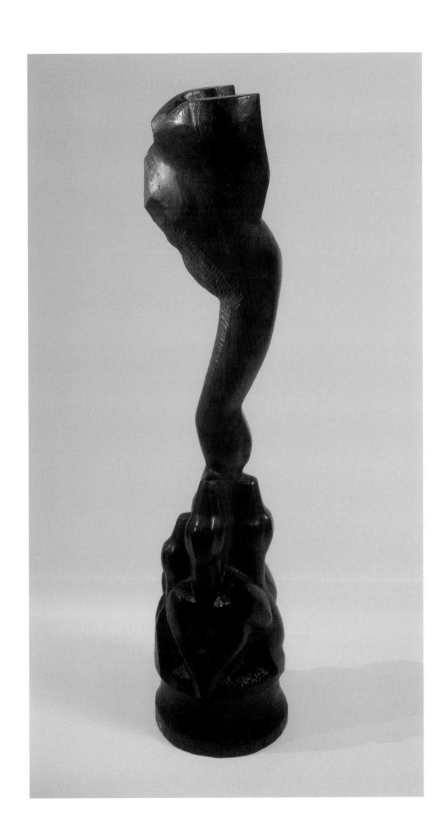

Acrobatic Performers, 1942

MAHOGANY

37½"H X 14"W X 1"D

Twins, 1943
SABICU WOOD
67"H X 13½"W X 11"D

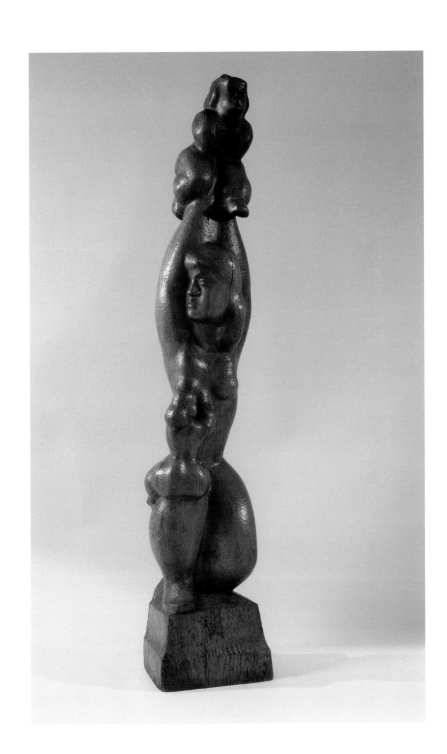

Swimmer, 1944
EBONY
10½"H X 46"L X 6½"D

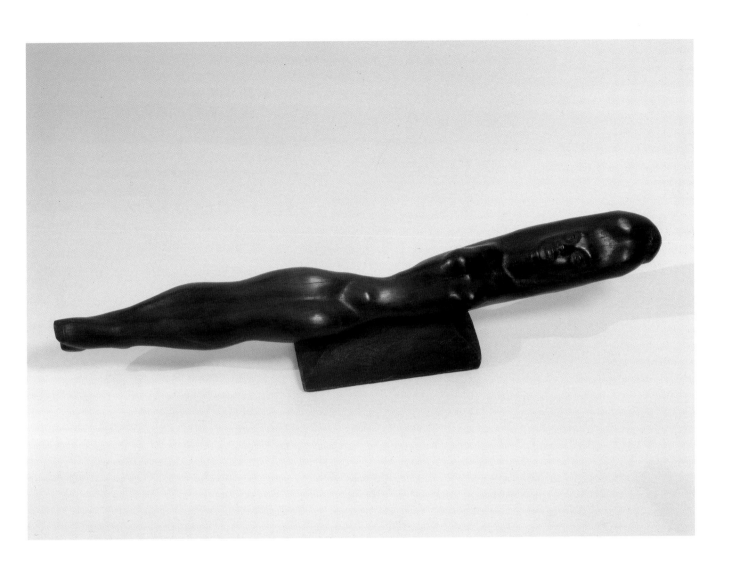

I Found My Love, 1948

MEXICAN TULIPWOOD

78"H X 10"W X 12"D

Head of a Girl, 1954
EBONY
9½"H X 6"W X 5"D

Sarah, 1956

LIGNUM VITAE

51½"H X 9½"W X 11"D

Head of a Girl, 1956
LIGNUM VITAE
12½"H X 6"W X 6"D

Balancing on a Unicycle, 1956
EBONY
42½"H X 11½"W X 7"D

The Hennenford Family, Acrobats, 1981
COCOBOLO WOOD
31½"H X 1½"W X 4"D